THE GREAT
IQ
CHALLENGE

THE GREAT
IQ
CHALLENGE

**PHILIP J.CARTER &
KEN A. RUSSELL**

**JOINT EDITORS OF THE MENSA UK
PUZZLE GROUP JOURNAL**

WARD LOCK

A WARD LOCK BOOK

First published in the UK
1994 by Ward Lock
Villiers House
41/47 Strand
LONDON
WC2N 5JE

A Cassell Imprint

Distributed in the United States
by Sterling Publishing Co., Inc.
387 Park Avenue South, New York, NY 10016-8810

Distributed in Australia
by Capricorn Link (Australia) Pty Ltd
2/13 Carrington Road, Castle Hill NSW 2154

A British Library Cataloguing in Publication Data block for this book may
be obtained from the British Library

ISBN 0-7063-7230-1

Design, typesetting and illustration Ben Cracknell

Printed and bound in Great Britain by Cox & Wyman Ltd, Reading

CONTENTS

ACKNOWLEDGEMENTS

We are indebted to our wives, both named Barbara, for their continued enthusiastic support in all our projects. Also to the members of Enigmasig for their support, interest, inspiration and lively correspondence. Our special thanks go to Lynn Moore for her contribution in typing the manuscript.

ABOUT THE AUTHORS

Philip Carter is an engineering estimator and also a Yorkshire JP. He is Editor of *Enigmasig*, the Mensa Special Interest Puzzle Group newsletter.

Ken Russell is a retired London surveyor and is also Puzzle Editor of *Mensa*, the monthly publication of British Mensa Limited.

INTRODUCTION

We are delighted to present the fifth book of puzzles in our IQ Challenge series, which started in 1986 with the first publication, *Take the IQ Challenge*. Our continued aim in this series has been to devise new types of interesting and challenging puzzles and to explore other puzzle-related topics. Our partnership as compilers began in 1983 through our membership of Mensa, the High-IQ Society, and, in particular, through our involvement with the appropriately named Enigmasig, the Special Interest Group of British Mensa Ltd, which is dedicated to the setting and solving of puzzles.

Mensa, the best known of the world's High-IQ societies, has a worldwide membership in excess of 100,000. Mensa is the Latin word for 'table', indicating a round table society, in which members, although holding widely differing views, are all equal in status. Although many individual opinions are expressed, no one member, or group of members, is allowed to express opinions on behalf of the society. The only criterion for membership is to have attained a score in a supervised IQ test that will put the applicant in the top 2 per cent of the population. The qualifying figure in the UK is a score of 148 on the Cattell scale of intelligence.

If you are interested in joining Mensa or in finding out your own IQ level, you should contact one of the addresses below. The procedure is that you will be given the opportunity of taking a test in the privacy of your own home. After this, if the results are sufficiently encouraging, you will be invited to sit in a supervised test at one of the sessions that are held regularly. If your score is within the qualifying level at this supervised test you will be sent an invitation to join the society and will immediately be on an equal standing with all other members.

UK
British Mensa Ltd
Mensa House
St John's Square
Wolverhampton
WV2 4AH

INTERNATIONAL
Mensa International Ltd
15 The Ivories
6–8 Northampton Street
London
N1 2HY

USA
American Mensa Ltd
2626 E14 Street
Brooklyn
NY 11235–3992

AUSTRALIA
Australian Mensa Inc.
PO BOX 519
Mona Vale
NSW 2103

ABOUT THE PUZZLES

So that you can monitor your performance we have allocated one of the following star ratings to each puzzle:

★ Standard
★ ★ More challenging
★ ★ ★ Difficult
★ ★ ★ ★ Incredibly difficult

You will see that each puzzle has been cross-referenced with two numbers – a question number (Q) and an answer number (A). This has enabled us to mix up the answers section so that there is no risk of your seeing the answer before you tackle the next puzzle.

WARM-UPS

All intellectual improvement arises from leisure.
                                              Samuel Johnson

This first section is a microcosm of the book as a whole, with a selection of puzzles designed to give you a flavour of what is to follow and, perhaps, to give you some hint as to how our devious minds work. We make no apology for trying to keep you on your toes by springing the unexpected on you every so often, so do remember not always to look for the obvious.

All our books are intended as a leisurely diversion from life's pressures, but at the same time we hope our tests and teasers will increase your intellectual prowess.

Good luck and happy solving!

Q1	★	A45
	Train Trip	

Between 60 and 100 people hired a private carriage for a railway trip and they paid a total of £3,895. Each person paid the same amount, which was an exact number of pounds. How many people went on the trip?

Four Numbers

The sums of four numbers, omitting each of the numbers in turn, are 22, 24, 27 and 20. What are the four numbers?

Two Numbers

Two numbers are such that if the first receives 30 from the second they are in the ratio 2 : 1, but if the second receives 50 from the first, their ratio is 1 : 3.

What are the two numbers?

Keyword

You are looking for a nine-letter word answer to this riddle.

My one to four comes every way,
My four to six resort for play,
My six to eight will imitate,
My one to three bang up-to-date,
My five to nine is flat in sheets,
My all can be paid for in the streets.

Prefix

Find a four-letter word that will fit in front of all these endings.

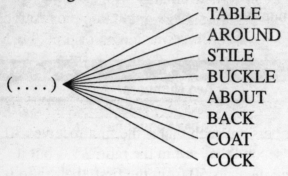

(. . . .)

TABLE
AROUND
STILE
BUCKLE
ABOUT
BACK
COAT
COCK

Codeword

Which word is missing from the second set of brackets?

BELONG (RUMBLE) ARMOUR
ANIMAL (. . . . . .) CAMBER

Reserves

In a game of eight players lasting for 50 minutes, two reserves alternate equally with each player. This means that all players, including the reserves, are on the pitch for the same length of time. For how long?

Number Sequences

In each of the following find the next number in the sequence.

1. 27834, 11132, 2226, 1332
2. 116, 128, 146, 161, 278
3. 125, 150, 215, 240, 305, 330, 355

Three Letters

WAS, TEN, PEN

Which of the following words has something in common with the three words above?

RIP, MAR, END, LIP, ZIP

Replace the Vowels

All of the vowels have been removed from the saying below. The consonants are in the correct order, but they have been broken up into groups of four. Replace the vowels and reconstitute the saying.

TSTP NTNT HRMN SSHS

Scrabble

What is the longest word that can be made from these 10 letters?

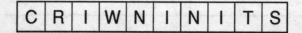

| C | R | I | W | N | I | N | I | T | S |

WORD GAMES

Playing with words is a universal activity. People delight in pulling words apart, reconstructing them in different guises, arranging them in clever patterns and finding hidden meanings within them. Although this section is dedicated entirely to word games, there are, in addition, many more different types of word play throughout the book.

We are confessed word game addicts, whether it is creating novel types of crossword grids, decoding or creating ingenious cryptic crossword clues or wrestling with the likes of chronograms, word squares, lipograms, palindromes, rebuses, heteronyms and homonyms. We never tire of searching for the unusual and are never bored by amazing facts – for example that Stanley Kimbrough of Chattanooga or Julie Schwarzkopf of Toledo are real people with 16-letter names with no repeats, and we take delight in discovering obscure items, such as that the longest word in the third edition of Webster's Dictionary without an 'e' is 'macracanthrorhynchiasis' – and we marvel that 'it's SOS read in flags' is an anagram of 'a signal of distress' and that 'sit not at ale bars' is an anagram of 'total abstainers'.

For us the English language is a bottomless treasure chest of delight, and we take great pleasure in creating chaos, for that is what a puzzle compiler is – a creator of chaos – but we hope that you derive equal pleasure in sorting out the chaos and that you are able to have the satisfaction of arriving at many of the correct answers.

Q12	★ ★ ★ ★	A85
	Tight Squeeze	

Place all the words listed below in the grid. Each word goes in the direction of a compass point, is in a straight line and starts and finishes in one of the shaded squares.

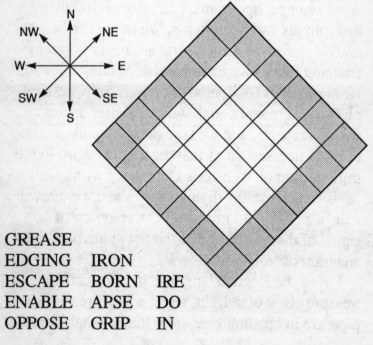

GREASE
EDGING   IRON
ESCAPE   BORN   IRE
ENABLE   APSE   DO
OPPOSE   GRIP   IN

Containers

Find a word and its container for each of the clues below – for example, Meat in a river = T(HAM)ES.

1. Incinerate in a tree
2. Monkey in a frolic
3. Injured in a battle
4. Behind in a weapon
5. Drink in a dance
6. Snooze in a drink
7. Circle in a confection
8. Transversely in a sport
9. Horizontal in a President
10. And the rest in a vegetable

Bracket Word

Place two letters in each bracket so that these finish the word on the left and start the word on the right. The letters in the brackets, read downwards in pairs, will spell out a 12-letter word.

GRA (..) ASE
T (..) US
W (..) CH
T (..) Y
PE (..) P
S (..) RE

Network 1

Trace out a 13-letter word by travelling along the lines. You must not cross a letter twice.

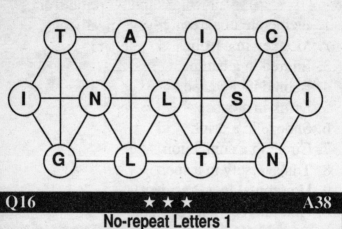

No-repeat Letters 1

The grid contains 25 different letters of the alphabet. What is the longest word that can be found by starting anywhere and working from square to square, horizontally, vertically or diagonally, and not repeating a letter?

L	P	R	F	J
I	T	Y	A	X
D	H	S	C	M
E	N	K	O	W
B	V	U	Q	G

No-repeat Letters 2

The grid contains 25 different letters of the alphabet. What is the longest word that can be found by starting anywhere and working from square to square, horizontally, vertically or diagonally, and not repeating a letter?

Y	D	Q	U	G
M	X	N	B	T
H	I	E	R	P
L	S	J	O	K
A	V	F	W	C

No-repeat Letters 3

The grid contains 25 different letters of the alphabet. What is the longest word that can be found by starting anywhere and working from square to square, horizontally, vertically or diagonally, and not repeating a letter.

F	I	Y	J	S
G	N	L	A	H
D	K	C	X	P
T	R	W	E	U
B	V	O	M	Q

The grid contains 25 different letters of the alphabet. What is the longest word that can be found by starting anywhere and working from square to square, horizontally, vertically or diagonally, and not repeating a letter?

G	L	Q	U	X
N	A	E	B	I
V	J	O	D	C
P	R	W	T	K
F	Y	M	H	S

The answers are all nine-letter words beginning with the letter G, and they are to be found in the grid, one letter on each line and in the correct order.

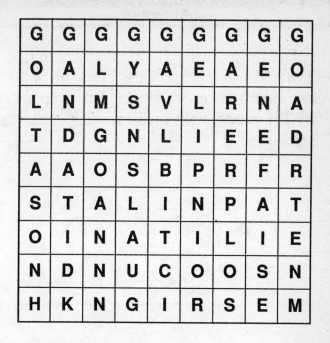

G	G	G	G	G	G	G	G	G
O	A	L	Y	A	E	A	E	O
L	N	M	S	V	L	R	N	A
T	D	G	N	L	I	E	E	D
A	A	O	S	B	P	R	F	R
S	T	A	L	I	N	P	A	T
O	I	N	A	T	I	L	I	E
N	D	N	U	C	O	O	S	N
H	K	N	G	I	R	S	E	M

1. Bird noted for singing
2. Walked by pirates
3. Tutor for children
4. Apparatus for producing electricity
5. Place for athletic training
6. Period of pregnancy
7. Horse moving quickly
8. Type of biscuit
9. Type of bag

Trackwords

In each of the following fill in the spaces to find
the two 15-letter words. All the letters are in the
correct order and the overlapping letter appears
twice. The words might appear reading clockwise
or anticlockwise.

1.

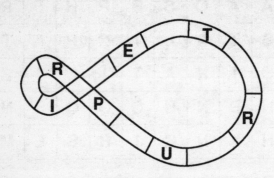

2.

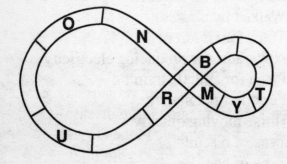

Novel Word Power

In the left-hand column is a list of words. The problem is to re-arrange these words so that their initial letters spell out the title of a book. To make the task easier, refer to the definitions in the centre column and put the correct word for each definition in the right-hand column. When all the words have been correctly placed, the book's title will appear when you read down the initial letters.

Words	Definitions	Answers
Tamp	Knowing or sly	
Lox	Reproach or censure	
Dulse	Relating to birds of prey	
Slough	A type of seaweed	
Leery	A small bird	
Houri	A white crystalline sugar	
Furbelow	To pack firmly	
Eyrir	Any alluring woman	
Opprobrium	An introductory part	
Impetigo	An ornamental trim	
Fructose	A kind of smoked salmon	
Ortolan	A contagious skin disease	
Exordium	An Icelandic monetary unit	
Raptorial	A hollow filled with mud	

Hexagonal Connections

With the help of the two letters already inserted, fit the 12 words into the spaces encircling the numbers in the hexagon so that each word correctly links with the two adjoining words. Some words will have to rotate clockwise and some anticlockwise.

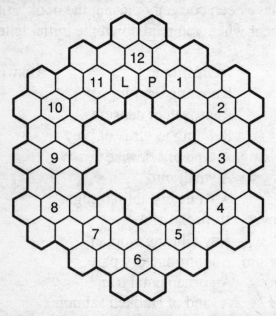

DORMER	TALLER	RIVALS
PORTAL	REMARK	TARGET
REMOVE	POPLAR	ARRIVE
GREASE	TRIPOD	SALLOW

Network 2

Find the starting point and travel along the connecting lines in a continuous path to adjacent circles to spell out a 14-letter word. Every circle must be visited once only.

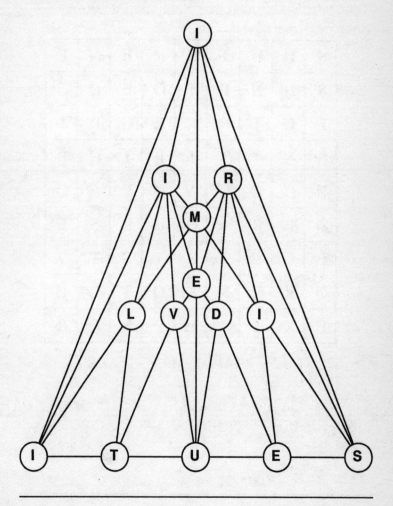

Jumble

Beginning always with the centre letter, W, travel from square to square in any direction, horizontally, vertically or diagonally, to spell out eight ll-letter words. Each letter is used once only.

S	H	U	T	E	R	E	N	E
S	H	N	E	T	G	E	D	G
E	C	T	R	N	R	G	R	I
R	N	I	I	I	E	I	H	B
U	D	L	O	W	H	E	E	O
O	L	R	A	O	H	R	S	E
L	C	E	T	R	I	S	T	V
O	R	L	N	K	O	T	L	E
E	K	I	A	M	P	S	E	R

Sixers

Place the correct letter in each circle to produce a six-letter word, reading clockwise.

1.
2.
3.

4.
5.
6.

Consonants

Restore the consonants to the words below which are all synonyms.

1. . E . . I . I . .
2. A . U . E . E . .
3. . O . . I . IA . I . .
4. . O . . I . I . A . I O .
5. . E . . I . E . .
6. . . E A . U . E
7. . E . E . . .
8. . A I E . .
9. . O . IA . I . .

LOGIC

Logic – the systematic study of inference.

The main requirement in solving the puzzles in this section is an ability to think logically. These puzzles are a test of your ability to reason correctly, and they are designed to stimulate both your intellect and your imagination.

One of our great puzzlist heroes, Charles Lutwidge Dodgson (Lewis Carroll) was a master logician, and as proof of this we are presenting one of his most famous logic problems, together with his reasoning towards arriving at a valid solution. It is a fine example of the kind of structured thinking necessary to solve many logic puzzles.

Statements

1. The only animals in this house are cats.
2. Every animal is suitable for a pet, that loves to gaze at the moon.
3. When I detest an animal, I avoid it.
4. No animals are carnivorous, unless they prowl at night.
5. No cat fails to kill mice.
6. No animal ever talks to me, except what are in this house.
7. Kangaroos are not suitable for pets.
8. None but carnivora kill mice.
9. I detest animals that do not talk to me.
10. Animals that prowl at night always love to gaze at the moon.

You have to deduce from this a unique conclusion.

Answer

Let the various types of animals mentioned in the statements be denoted by a single letter as follows: H = animals in the house; C = cats; P = animals suitable for pets; G = animals that love to gaze at the moon; D = animals that I detest; A = animals that I avoid; V = carnivorous animals; N = animals that prowl at night; M = killers of mice; T = animals that talk to me; K = kangaroos.

The 10 statements can now be expressed in symbolic form to highlight their logical structure as follows.

$P \rightarrow Q$ stands for: if P then Q

$-P$ stands for: not P

1. $H \rightarrow C$
2. $G \rightarrow P$
3. $D \rightarrow A$ and $-A \rightarrow -D$
4. $V \rightarrow N$
5. $C \rightarrow M$
6. $T \rightarrow H$
7. $K \rightarrow -P$ and $P \rightarrow -K$
8. $M \rightarrow V$
9. $T \rightarrow D$ and $-D \rightarrow T$
10. $N \rightarrow G$

All the statements can now be linked together in a chain of implications.

$$-A \rightarrow -D \rightarrow T \rightarrow H \rightarrow C \rightarrow M \rightarrow V \rightarrow N \rightarrow G \rightarrow P \rightarrow -K$$

Hence $-A \rightarrow -K$ or I avoid kangaroos.

Paths

Entering at A and without moving backwards or retracing your steps, how many different paths are there to B? There is a simple rule.

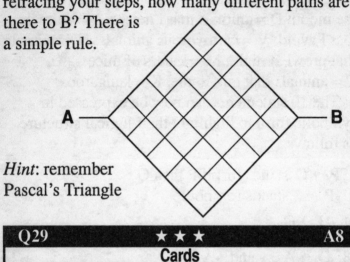

A — — **B**

Hint: remember Pascal's Triangle

Cards

Three men sat down to play cards, and nobody started with a fraction of a pound

1. Alan won from Bill as much as Alan had originally.
2. Bill won from Charlie as much as Bill then had left.
3. Charlie won from Alan as much as Charlie had left.
4. They ended up equal.
5. I began with £50.

Which of the three is speaking in the fifth statement?

Fribs and Twogs

A Frib is neither a Loji nor a Mith
A Twog is a Dork or a Nurf
A Gluc is neither a Caln nor a Josh
A Shen is a Loji or a Nurf
A Korl is neither a Dork nor a Nurf
A Brut is a Caln or a Josh
A Frib is a Josh or a Nurf
A Korl is a Josh

Which is which?

Coins

You are in a foreign country that has three types of coins.

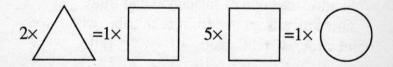

$2\times$ △ $=1\times$ □ $5\times$ □ $=1\times$ ○

You purchase a necklace with two coins, then you return to purchase four more necklaces with two coins. Which coins did you use for each purchase?

Scales

There were five entrants for the Enigma club boxing tournament. The entrants went on the scales two at a time, and every possible combination of two contestants was weighed, which gave $4 + 3 + 2 + 1 = 10$ separate weighings. These were recorded as 110kg, 112kg, 113kg, 114kg, 115kg, 116kg, 117kg, 118kg, 120kg and 121kg.

How much did each entrant to the tournament weigh?

Island

Three tribes live on an island. The 'truers' always tell the truth; the 'fibbers' always lie; and the 'trubers' make statements that alternate between truth and falsehood or falsehood and truth.

Three members, one from each tribe, whom we will call A, B and C, said:

A said C is a truer
B said A is a truer
C said nothing

To which tribes do A, B and C belong?

Cricketers

Three ex-England cricket captains were discussing their scores.

David said: I scored 9; I scored 2 fewer than Mike; I scored 1 more than Graham.

Mike said: I did not score the lowest; the difference between my score and Graham's was 3; Graham scored 12.

Graham said: I scored fewer runs than David; David scored 10; Mike scored 3 more than David.

If each man made one incorrect statement out of three, what were their scores?

Neighbours

Ten men live in a street. A, B, C, D and E live at numbers 1 – 5, and F, G, H, I and J live at numbers 6 – 10, but not necessarily in that order.

The man next door to the man opposite I is E.
F lives three houses away from G.
H lives opposite C.
If C is not central, then A is.
B lives three houses away from C.
If F is not central, then I is.
D lives opposite G.

1	2	3	4	5

10	9	8	7	6

The man next door to the man opposite A is J.
C does not live at number 5.

Where do they all live?

If mathematically you end up with the incorrect answer, try multiplying by the page number.

Murphy's Ninth Law

Mathematics is an exact science, and there is only one correct solution to a correctly set calculation or puzzle, although there may be different methods of arriving at that solution, some more laborious than others!

Approximation and improvisation, although unlikely to enable you to reach the exact solution, can be useful at times, however, as one of the authors of this book has demonstrated on a couple of occasions. Many years ago he attended a school fête with his two young daughters. Among the stalls was one where a competition was in progress to guess the number of sweets packed into a large jar. The author boasted that he had a secret formula whereby he could count the number of sweets down, across and deep, then multiply the three figures together and finally multiply by a decimal less than one, which he called the packaging factor, and so arrive at the correct number. Sure enough, when the results were announced, the author was the winner, being only one out in total. He claimed to his daughters that he had a secret and ancient book that gave the packaging factor. Untrue, of course, but many years later the system worked again when he went into a travel agents that were running a similar competition. He applied the same system, and, sure enough, received a telephone call that same evening to say that he was the winner, again only one out in total. The prize of a holiday for four was his.

We are now pleased to share this formula with you. Try it out at the next fête you attend. We would love to hear if you have been successful.

Sweets across   8
Sweets down   12
Sweets deep   6
Multiply $8 \times 12 \times 6 = 576 \times 0.8$
                              $= 460$ sweets in the jar

Magic Square

Place the remaining numbers from 1 – 25 in the grid so that each horizontal, vertical and corner-to-corner line totals 65.

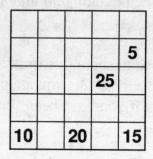

				5
		25		
10		20		15

Return Journey

If a car had covered a distance of 210 miles from A to B at an average speed of 5 mph faster than it did, the time for the journey would have been one hour less. What was its speed?

Connections

Insert the numbers 0 to 11 in the circles below so that, for any particular circle, the sum of the numbers in the circles connected directly to it equals the value corresponding to the number in that circle, as given in the list below.

Example
1=14 (4 + 7 + 3)
4=8 (7 + 1)
7=5 (4 + 1)
3=1

0=17
1=31
2=20
3=1
4=8
5=25
6=13
7=1
8=22
9=6
10=14
11=2

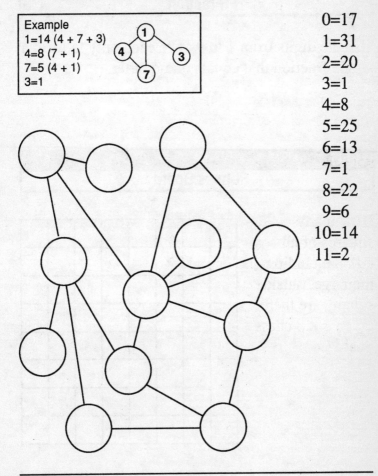

Round Table

In how many ways can a committee of seven be seated round a table?

Fraction

Use the digits from 1 to 9 once each only to form a single fraction that equals one-quarter.

Chess Board

How many squares of all sizes, including the large, outside square, are there on an 8×8 chess board?

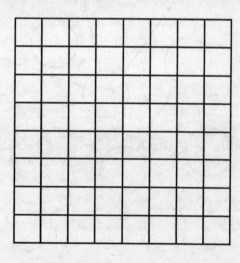

Three Words 1

1. In how many ways can the letters of the word 'paragons' be arranged?

2. Using all the letters of the word 'pound', in how many arrangements are the vowels separated?

3. In how many different ways can the letters in the word 'combine' be arranged so that no two vowels are adjacent?

The 38 Puzzle

Place the numbers 1 to 19 in the circles so that every straight row of three, four or five circles in any direction adds up to 38.

Ages

1. I have three children. The sum of their ages equals the age of my wife, and if I multiply the children's ages together the total is 1,200. My wife had her first child when she was 19 and our third child when she was 35. How old are the children and my wife?

2. The ages of my three daughters when multiplied together equal 1,800. The sum of their ages equals my age, which is a prime number. How old are we?

Squares?

What is the next term in this series?

100, 121, 144, 202, 244, 400

Square Numbers

Each horizontal and vertical line contains the digits of a different four-figure square number. In each line the four digits are always in the correct order, but they are not necessarily adjacent. All numbers in the grid are used once and once only. Find the 16 square numbers.

2	5	5	1	4	8	4	3
1	7	3	1	6	3	9	4
1	6	3	3	7	1	2	1
1	8	9	6	6	0	2	4
1	2	2	6	5	3	1	4
4	8	2	2	2	2	5	8
8	9	8	9	4	3	6	6
6	6	9	5	6	6	1	1

LOONY LAWS

The Cassell English Dictionary defines Sod's Law as 'A wry maxim that anything which can possibly go wrong will do so' (short for Sodomite).

Sod's is perhaps the most widely quoted of this type of maxim, but there are many more similarly loony laws (or truisms), which you can use as either mere amusement, talking points or guides to your lifestyle. A few examples from our collection are:

Nothing is as easy as it looks. Everything takes longer than you expect. If anything can go wrong, it will do so, and always at the worst possible moment.   *Murphy's Law*

The least experienced fisherman always catches the biggest fish.
                    Porkingham's Third Law of Sport Fishing

The more elaborate and costly the equipment, the greater the chance of having to stop at the fish market on the way home.   *Corollary*

If you do something that you are sure will meet with everybody's approval, somebody won't like it.   *Chisholm's First Corollary*

If you perceive that there are four possible ways in which a procedure can go wrong and circumvent these, a fifth will promptly develop.

Murphy's Law of Multiples

Dimensions will always be expressed in the least usable terms. Velocity, for example, will always be expressed in furlongs per fortnight.

Van Troy's Law

Don't ever stand up to be counted or someone will take your seat   *Eagle's Law*

An unbreakable toy is good for breaking other toys.   *Jason's Law*

A road map always tells you everything except how to refold it.   *Grandma's Observation*

The number of laws will expand to fill the publishing space available.   *Digiovanni's Law*

There are 10 more trite sayings and loony laws to find in this section, which will no doubt be an especial source of great delight to the cynics among you.

Boling's Postulate

If you're feeling good, don't worry you'll soon get over it.

Using all 45 letters of the above quotation once each only, complete the pyramid with one one-letter word, one two-letter word, one three letter word and so on.

Clues are given, but they are in no particular order.

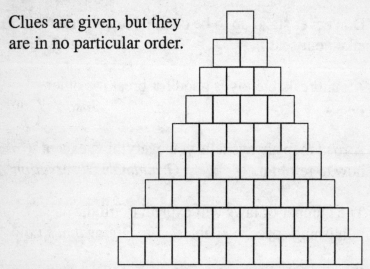

Clues:

A type of black magic

Frighten

The chemical symbol for tungsten

Warbling in a falsetto tone

Web-footed bird

Passing

The person addressed

Alternatively

Move round

Cann's Axiom

Find the first letter and, travelling from square to square in any direction, horizontally, vertically or diagonally, spell out a trite saying. Every letter is used, but only once, and the sentence ends at a square next to the asterisk.

R	C	T	I	O	S
U	T	S	N	N	*
D	T	E	I	H	E
A	E	H	W	N	A
R	S	F	E	L	L
L	I	A	S	L	E

Agnes's Law

A trite saying has been split into groups of three letters, which have then been arranged in alphabetical order. Re-arrange the groups of three letters to restore the saying.

. . . .
. .   . .

ALM, EAS, ElS, ETI, EVE, GIN, HIN, IER, LIF, NOU, NTO, OST, RYT, THA, TOF, TOG

Ponemon's Provocation

Move around the circle and select letters to a definite pattern to spell out a trite saying. Each letter is used once. The problem is to find the starting point. The saying appears in a clockwise direction.

Finagle's Law and Chisholme's Law

Below are two loony laws fused together. All the letters are in the correct order. Can you find the two laws? Once you find one the other will automatically appear. For example, Finagle and Chisholme fused together might appear as FCIHINSHAGOLLMEE.

ONANCYTEIMAJETOHBINIGSSAFOPULPEE
ARDUTPOBEEVEGROYINTHGINBEGTDOTE
NRETYOOIUMHPRAVOVEOEIVTOERNLLOY
OMKEADKSOESIMETWOTRHSINEG.

Feldstein's Law

Complete the crossword and place the words in the correct order to find a trite saying.

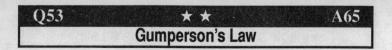

Gumperson's Law

The following is a straightforward cryptogram in which each letter of the alphabet has been replaced by another.

JUA YTBLFLPGPJD BH FQDJUPQM
UFYYAQPQM PC PQ PQNATCA
YTBYBTJPBQ JB PJC RACPTFLPGPJD

Murphy's Twelfth Law

Start at the section indicated by the arrow and then select words in the correct order from anywhere within the wheel to find a loony law.

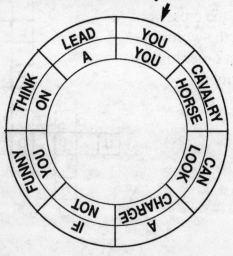

Blomgren's Law

Find the starting point and then, using the knight's move as in chess (see diagram), spell out the message.

Knight's Move

Y	A	H	S	S
E	I	H	L	T
E	P	T	I	A
Y	S	R	O	I

Intelligence – the ability to respond adaptively to novel situations.

Logical reasoning is again the requirement for solving the puzzles in this section. These are what we describe as 'puzzles of the mind', and they consist entirely of diagrammatic representation. They are not puzzles of numeracy or literacy but are 'culture fair' tests, free from the influence of prior knowledge. Many regard this type of test as the most accurate way of measuring pure intelligence.

To solve these puzzles a great deal of lateral thinking is required. If you cannot solve them immediately, do not be tempted to go straight to the answer. Instead, let your subconscious go to work and return to the puzzle some time later. It is surprising how quickly the answer often comes at the second or even third attempt.

Sequence

Which of the options – A, B, C, D or E –
continues the sequence?

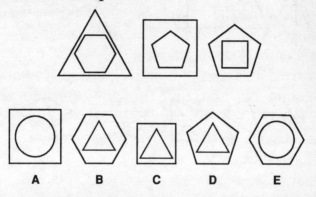

A   B   C   D   E

Quartering a Square

Divide the grid
below into four
sections, each of
the same shape
and size and each
containing one
each of the five
different
symbols.

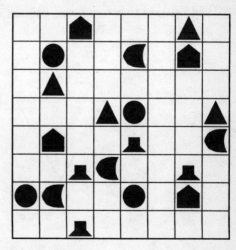

Analogy

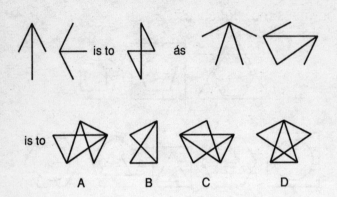

Two Hexagons

Divide the star into seven pieces to produce two hexagons.

Matrix 1

Find the missing tile.

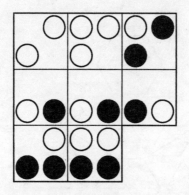

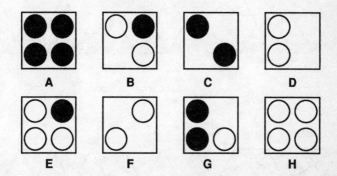

Hexagonal Pyramid

Which hexagon – A, B, C, D or E – should appear at the top of the pyramid?

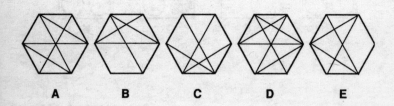

A   B   C   D   E

Matrix 2

Find the missing tile.

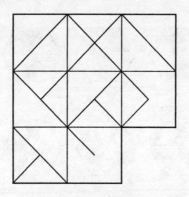

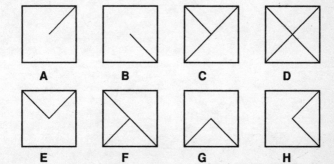

Hexagons

Which hexagon – A, B, C, D or E – completes the sequence.

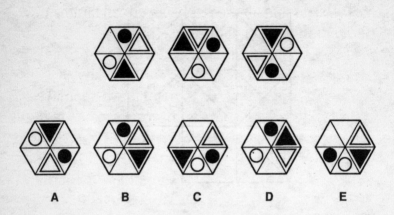

A   B   C   D   E

ANAGRAMS

In his 1903 book *The Handy Book of Literary Curiosities,* the English author William Walsh wrote: 'After centuries of endeavour, so few really good anagrams have been rolled down to us. One may assert that all the really superb anagrams now extant might be contained in a pillbox.'

Since then, the fascination for anagrams has never waned, and one can be sure that any politician, entertainer or sportsman who achieves fame will find the letters of his or her name being massaged into numerous permutations in the search for the perfect anagram.

In the November 1990 issue of the US Journal of Recreational Linguistics, *Word Ways*, O.V. Michaelson considered the criteria available for judging the quality of an anagram. 'That's prime news? No, it preys on the week' (The newspaper is not the New York Times), he argued, is deficient because it must be explained that it refers to a New York weekly that regards sensationalism as 'prime' news. Similarly, unnecessary words detract from the theme, as 'the Great' and 'the Late, Great' in the anagrams 'the good man, he lit vast areas' (the Great Thomas Alva Edison) and 'think tall – a dreamer greeting truth' (the Late Great Dr Martin Luther King).

So, what is the ultimate anagram? Perhaps there

is no better example than Melvin O. Wellman's classic of 1948, 'eleven + two = twelve + one'. It is perfect in that it is completely transposed and grammatically correct and meets the purists' rule that an anagram should never contain more than three letters in the same sequence.

Here is a selection of classic anagrams that have appeared in the twentieth century.

Cleopatra's Needle, London – An old lone stone replaced   (*Chambers Journal, 1900*)

Gold and silver – Grand old evils
(*J. Hentry Wickham, 1903*)

The Metropolitan Opera House – Theatre to harmonious people   (*F.W. Dougherty,, 1906*)

Surgical instruments – Smart curing utensils
(*F.M. Walling, 1915*)

The American Indian – I am in a thinned race
(*Howard B. McPherrin, 1924*)

A decimal point – I'm a dot in place
(*Helen M. Miller, 1928*)

Western Union – No wire unsent
(*L.D. Rees, 1931*)

The Desert Oasis – Does ease thirst
(*David Shulman, 1936*)

An aisle – Is a lane   (*Patrick J. Flavin, 1939*)

The countryside – No city dust here
(*Susan Eagleton, 1948*)

One good turn deserves another – Do rogues
   endorse that? No never   (*Leigh Mercer, 1953*)

The assassination of President Abraham Lincoln –
   A pistol in an actor's rebel hands, a fine man
   is shot   (*Jessie McPherrin, 1959*)

The cardinals – In cathedrals
                        (*author unknown, 1965*)

The complete works of William Shakespeare –
   Pick Marlow: ask if he wrote all these poems
                        (*Lindon Bosson, 1978*)

Clint Eastwood – Old West action
                        (*author unknown, 1984*)

The good Samaritans – Hearts go to man's aid
                        (*Loris B. Curtis, 1989*)

Chrissie Evert – It's her service
                        (*author unknown, 1990*)

In this section we present a selection of word
games, all on an anagrammatic theme.

Anagrammed Synonyms

Study the following list of three words. Your task is to find the two of the three words that can be paired to form an anagram of one word, which is a synonym of the word remaining. For example, in the group LEG – MEEK– NET, the words LEG and NET are an anagram of GENTLE, which is a synonym of the remaining word, MEEK.

1. RAP– OUR– DIN
2. ERA– RUB– DAB
3. HOAX – CEDE – POINT
4. BULL– EGO – DROP
5. SAIL– LONE– DOTE
6. SHIP– ROAM – SAW
7. SANG – BLEEP– STUD
8. CREED – WAY – POUR
9. NOTE – STEP – LIE
10. TIE– ERR– STAIN

Anagram Magic Square

Tiny lanterns nail a test sale.

Using all 25 letters in the sentence above, form five five-letter words that when placed correctly in the grid, will form a magic word square in which all five words can be read both horizontally and vertically.

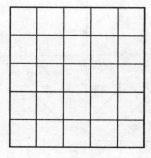

The Enigmasig Wheel

Complete the word in each column. All the words end in E, and the scrambled letters in the section to the right of each column are an anagram of a word that will provide a clue to the word you are trying to find to fit in the column.

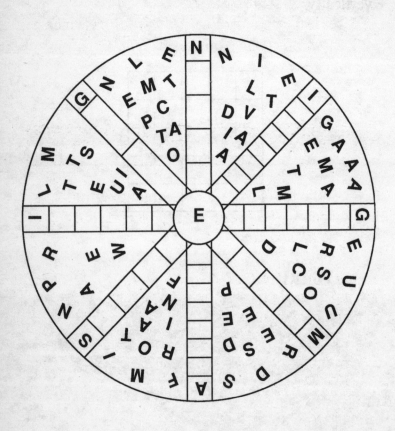

Reverse Anagram

If we presented you with the words MAR, AM and FAR and asked you to find the shortest English word that contained all the letters from which these words could be produced, we would expect you to come up with the word FARM. Here is a further list of words: STRIDE, TAX, MOUSE and BOARD.

What is the shortest English word from which all these words can be produced?

Anagram Phrases

Each of the following is an anagram of a well-known phrase. For example, SO NOTE HOLE = ON THE LOOSE.

1. TOO BRIGHT GLINT
2. TAP TOP EARTH, O LOOK DO IT!
3. BITE OTHER CAKE
4. EVADES SLY IN DENS
5. F.A.O. BRIDE'S FATHER

Pyramid Words 1

Solve the five clues, place the five words in the pyramid, then re-arrange all 15 letters to find a 15-letter word.

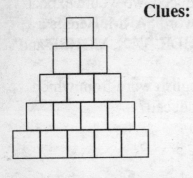

Clues: The sixth note of the diatonic scale of C major (1)
Within (2)
20cwt (3)
Large town (4)
The place where a battle is fought (S)

Pyramid Words 2

Solve the five clues, place the five words in the pyramid, then re-arrange all 15 letters to find a 15-letter word.

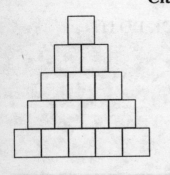

Clues: The third note of the diatonic scale (1)
Refusal (2)
Fruit with hard shell (3)
Kill (4)
Discolour (5)

Anagram Themes

In each of the following arrange the 14 words in pairs so that each pair is an anagram of another word or name. The seven words produced will have a linking theme. For example, if the words TRY and CREASE were in the list, they could be paired to form an anagram of SECRETARY and the theme could be professions.

1. THEN, RAP, ODE, CRY, ALBUM, HER, WORD, COSY, LAP, CUTS, RUN, MARE, LOP, ME

2. END, THE, LIE, ELM, MAID, HE, BAR, RAN, BAIL, SAIL, RUM, DEN, HEAR, HAT

REBUSES

Rebus – the enigmatic representation in visual form of the sounds of a name or word.

Rebus is a Latin word meaning 'by things', indicating a coded text, which can be deciphered by studying its visual display.

Rebuses first became popular in Mensa circles during the mid- to late 1970s with such teasers as those illustrated here, the

GNIKOOL 1978 1979 1980	THE & EEEEEEE

answers to which are 'looking backward over the years' and 'the Andes'.

More recently they have become popular features in newspapers and magazines, and they are the basis of the popular television quiz show *Catchphrase*. Traditional rebuses, such as the one illustrated here – Panda – use illustrations, but some

P	✋	H
		A

modern rebuses use letters or arrangements of letters such as $\frac{DES}{DES}$ (despair) or 18U (I hate you).

Some rebuses have become part of everyday writing, such as IOU (I owe you), and they are

found in ancient means of communication, such as hieroglyphics, ancient pictography, such as that used in the early Minoan period in

Crete, and modern pictography, such as road signs.

We first used rebuses in our 1986 publication *Take the IQ Challenge*, and they proved very popular, one reader comparing them with Rorschach inkblot tests. We are, therefore, reintroducing them by popular demand in this book, and 60 newly compiled ones follow in this section. The answers may be just one word or a well-known phrase.

1. **TOP**	2. **FOTIL**	3. **NONONOIIIIIIII**
4. **_ AK _**	5. **BIBLE**	6. **TRUFNOSE**
7. **ON** **I**	8. **TTTTTT**	9. **R** **I N A** **B**
10. **T** **A** **RGE** **T**	11. **HANDE**	12. **TH_ W_Y OF _L_ _LESH**

Rebuses 2

1. T N U R	2. **FUR**	3. APOPORKERKE
4. TURPIN	5. **TOP** **THE**	6. zzzz
7. **FORWELLMED**	8. A M L E P	9. **GLI**
10. S H P O	11. **NMUTUA**	12. **DESKEP**

69

1. XQQQ	2. Hz	3. $0.01
4. M I C K JAGGER	5. PATELLA LAMP	6. CROISSA
7. P A S SION	8. TUASPRF	9. WELL
10. MUCH A D O	11. ✔.	12. ATLOALSIKEA

1. SESTICKCT	2. E A G L E	3. P E RSO N
4. _ _ _ _OSE	5. M I N D S	6. OLD BAILEY
7. HARMONY	8.	9. 9999 0 0 1
10. _I_ _Y _ _ _U_ _ _	11. LEVEL LEVEL	12. AALLLL

Rebuses 5

1. WHEELS	2. **12.00**	3. AS TAT EOF
4. POCILY	5. PORTTAXUGAL	6. _TOR_
7. STRE ETS	8. UPLATM	9. S U I T
10. AVI	11. JOL ◆ SON	12. THE FIFTHE

BRAINBENDERS

One of the authors of this book visited California recently and went to the State Fair, where a famous old brain-bender game was in progress. The punters had to place a wager with the barker that they could cover one large black disc with five smaller discs. The barker first demonstrated how easy it was and then offered the discs to the spectators. Needless to say, nobody ever won, the reason being that unknown to the spectators the barker had cleverly substituted slightly smaller discs for the discs he had used in the demonstration. The mathematics of this game are that unless the small discs have a diameter of at least 0.618034 of the larger disc it cannot be done.

This decimal 0.618034 is called the 'golden section' or 'golden mean', and it is a proportion obtained if a point P divides a straight line AB in such manner that AP:PB = AB:AP. It is often denoted by (τ) and, like pi (π), τ is irrational, having no finite value.

AP : PB = AB : AP

The Fibonacci numbers also lead to this remarkable number, which often occurs in nature and is seemingly nature's way of economically spacing out and packing objects. It was also applied to architecture by Vitruvius in the first century BC and much discussed during the Renaissance. Pietro della Francesca's *Baptism of Christ* (National Gallery, London) is just one example of a composition set up according to this proportion.

The Fibonacci sequence dates from AD 1202, when Leonardo of Pisa (Fibonacci) propounded the following puzzle in his *Liber Abaci* (*Book of the Abacus*): beginning with a single pair, how many pairs of rabbits will be produced in a year, if in every month each pair bears a new pair, which becomes productive from the second month on? The sequence that solves this puzzle is the now famous Fibonacci sequence: 0, 1, 1, 2, 3, 5, 8, 13, 34, 55, 89, 144, 233, 377, 610, 987, etc, in which each number is the sum of the previous two. If we pair these numbers into fractions and convert them into decimals, we converge on the golden ratio 0.618034. For example:

$$\frac{21}{34} = 0.617647$$

$$\frac{34}{55} = 0.618182$$

$$\frac{55}{89} = 0.617978$$

$$\frac{89}{144} = 0.618056$$

$$\frac{144}{233} = 0.618026$$

$$\frac{233}{377} = 0.618037$$

$$\frac{377}{610} = 0.618032$$

$$\frac{610}{987} = 0.618034$$

We wonder if the fairground barker is aware that his artful enterprise has its origins deep in the history of mathematics.

It is now time for you to roll up your sleeves, not to get to grips with impossible fairground games, but to tackle the selection of puzzles that follow in this section. These puzzles have just one thing in common – their high degree of difficulty.

Four Letters

Which four letters come next in this sequence?

AMON, AJUN, APHO, ALIT, CSAC

No Zeros

How can 1,000,000,000 be written as the product of two factors), neither of which contains any zeros at all ?

Sea Level

A man who is six feet tall stands on a beach. How far out to sea can he see?

Brain Strain

Insert the missing numbers so that the calculations are correct, both across and down. All numbers to be inserted are less than 10, and there is no zero.

	x		-		=	4
+		x		÷		x
	+		+	2	=	
÷		÷		-		÷
	x	2	-		=	
=		=		=		=
2	+		÷		=	

Dominoes

A complete set of 28 dominoes has been laid out in the grid below. Draw in the lines to show how the 28 dominoes have been arranged.

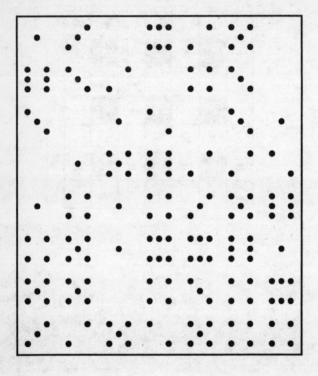

16 Letters

Divide the square into four identical sections, each of which contains the same 16 letters, which can be arranged into a well-known phrase.

K	A	N	W	L	K	A	L
A	N	E	R	N	A	H	W
R	W	E	N	O	E	H	W
E	E	N	W	K	L	A	S
P	S	L	O	O	H	W	P
W	H	E	P	L	N	E	K
S	L	W	A	E	N	S	P
R	O	A	L	N	L	R	A

Cartwheels

The front wheel of a cart makes four revolutions more than the rear wheel over a distance of 120 yards. If the circumference of each wheel were reduced by 3 feet, the front wheel would make six revolutions more than the rear wheel over the same distance.

What where the original circumferences of the two wheels?

Number Crunching

Most calculators only have up to eight digits available so this is more of a number-crunching problem than a puzzle. Nevertheless, it is included because of the interesting feature that the answer produces.

What do the cubes of the two numbers 4464658829 and 871517841 have in common?

Directional Numbers

Place all the numbers listed below into the grid. Each number goes in the direction of a compass point, is in a straight line and starts and finishes in one of the shaded squares.

375624 71538
289933 32146
896421 16672
466112 11221
291283 9173
888 9218

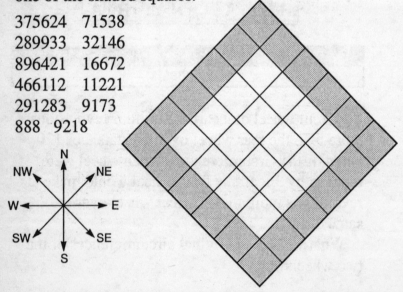

The 20 10-letter Word Boggle

Work from square to square, horizontally, vertically or diagonally, to spell out 20 10-letter words. The words are spelt out in pairs of letters, and every square must be used. It does not matter which word you identify first. As long as you make the correct turnings you will eventually return to your starting point. No square is used more than once.

PR	OP	ER	LN	VU	TO	IN	RM	TE	DE
RI	TE	AB	LE	UM	RI	DI	ED	IC	ST
ET	NA	MI	PP	DI	NT	AU	EX	CI	LA
OR	IL	LU	OI	SA	RT	ME	TE	HO	SC
PA	SM	LI	NT	WO	HW	MA	RK	AB	LE
UL	RT	NA	UR	ES	OR	HI	RE	LE	NG
AR	IC	JO	TR	CH	US	RO	LE	AD	RA
BE	PS	AL	RM	ID	AB	TE	BO	QU	CE
ED	DE	YC	FO	LE	OP	IS	ST	EN	UL
LL	VI	HO	LO	GY	TI	MI	IC	TU	RB

KICKSELF

A good kickself is a puzzle that, if you cannot solve it, you want to kick yourself immediately you see the solution because you cannot understand why you did not think of it. It is not a kickself if you think 'well, I would never have thought of that' because it is either too obscure or too complicated, or it involves specialist knowledge. As examples of this look at the next two puzzles. The first, Q87, is a good kickself because it involves something of which almost everyone who picks up this book will be familiar, but the second, Q88, although it is a good puzzle, is perhaps not such a good kickself because it involves knowledge of a certain fact, with which not so many people will be familiar.

Kickself puzzles are said to have originated in 1980 at a lunch in Cambridge attended by the Mensa President, Victor Serebriakoff, British Mensa Chairman, Sir Clive Sinclair, and Arthur C. Clarke, the renowned science fiction author. Arthur C. Clarke asked: 'What was the first human artefact to break the sound barrier?' There was a brief pause before Clive Sinclair gave the correct answer 'a whip', the tip makes a small sonic boom (the crack) as it passes through Mach 1.

The following puzzles are all designed to inflict sore shins!

Find the smallest number that makes the following a palindromic sequence:

6, 9, 2, 4, 1, 8, 11

There are 362880 different possible nine-digit numbers that can be formed using the digits 1, 2, 3, 4, 5, 6, 7, 8 and 9 once only. How many of these are prime numbers?

Move the position of just one of the words below so that all the words are in alphabetical sequence.

PREACH, ABSORB, ERUPT, IONIC, AXIAL, ABYSMAL

Something in Common

What do these numbers have in common?

789	963	654
951	7410	852
620	753	321

Sharon's Telegram

What is the name of the person who let Norah see Sharon's telegram?

Coal Overboard

A ship loaded with coal sits in a closed dock. The coal is thrown overboard into the water. Will the water level on the wall of the dock rise, fall or remain the same?

Decimals

What comes next in this sequence?

1.000, 1.414, 1.732, 2.000, 2.236, 2.449

Key Sequence

The safe can only be opened by using the keys in the correct order that spells out a word. What is that word? Every key must be used just once.

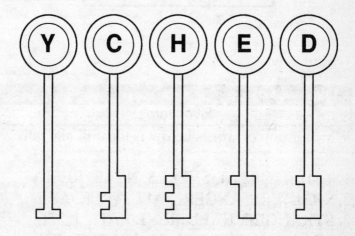

The Lake

The lake has been enclosed by a fence that is in two sets of parallel lines forming a rectangle touching the lake at points S.

Can you fence the lake with a fence formed in a square that touches the lake at four points?

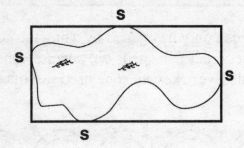

Five Words

Which group of words below is the odd one out?

1. TREAT, GREAT, SHELLS, NEAR, REEL
2. SHELTERS, ANGER, TALL, TREE, ARE
3. STRANGER, HALL, REST, RATE, LATE
4. LEARN, SHEER, LARGE, LATTER, SET

Silli Billis

One thousand, two hundred, nothing and one, transposed, give a word expressive of fun. What is that word?

Topiary

An aeroplane flying over a garden when a man was doing topiary work was astonished to find a message from him. What was the message?

Railway Wagon

A wagon on a frictionless track at the sidings is half-filled with water. The valve in the partition is opened by remote control. Will the wagon: remain still, move left and keep moving, move to the left and stop, move to the right and keep moving, or move to the right and stop?

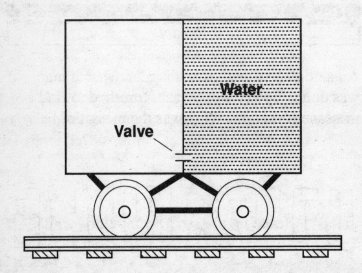

CRYPTOGRAMS

Cryptography is the alteration of the form of a message by codes and ciphers to conceal its meaning All the cryptograms in this brief section are straightforward cryptograms in which each letter of the alphabet has been substituted by another letter or symbol, and several involve finding an additional coded message.

The deciphering of the message is called cryptoanalysis. The practical use of codes and ciphers is to protect sensitive information from falling into the hands of enemies or rivals. It is necessary first to intercept the message, then to analyse it to reveal its contents. An important consideration is the different frequencies with which letters of the alphabet occur – in English, the order in which letters appear most frequently is ETAOINSRHLDCUMFPGWYBVKXJQZ – and the prime task is to search for such enciphered patterns. In recent years this process has been greatly assisted by the use of computers, which has necessitated the need to devise even more sophisticated codes.

Cryptogram

This is a straight substitution cryptogram in which each letter of the alphabet has been substituted by another.

ZVSC IC PJC DWYWGVCU MO DVOC
EFQ V KVDD KVDDVFZDB QM
KVPJMWP PJC FCNCUUVPVCU.

OGEFT DDMBQ KGVZJP

Numbergram

This is a straight substitution cryptogram in which each letter of the alphabet has been substituted by a number corresponding to its position in the alphabet – i.e., A = 1, B = 2, etc. The problem is to find not only the starting and finishing point of the letters but of the words, too. For instance, 'SOLVE THE CRYPTOGRAM', which is represented by the numbers 19, 15, 12, 22, 5   20, 8, 5   3, 18, 25, 16, 20, 15, 7, 18, 1, 3 would appear as: 191512225208531825162015571813.

23151811524161144191915119201569121220852
09145122191212125615189201931513161252 09
1514.

325189121415182083152051611811914191514

90

Cryptosymbol

Decode the following.

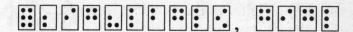

Cryptokey I

	1	2	3	4
A	A		
B	B		
C	C		
D	D		
E	E		
F	F		
G	G		
H	H		
I	I		
J	J		
K	K		
L	L		
M	M		
N	N		
O	O		
P	P		
Q	Q		
R	R		
S	S		
T	T		
U	U		
V	V		
W	W		
X	X		
Y	Y		
Z	Z		

Start by solving the cryptogram that follows, which is a straightforward code in which each letter of the alphabet has been replaced by another.

CJOG KG IJNI JHAPO WXP
RKBKRO KS IJOE'BO N QZNKG
NGR MOZOQOVVAW IHH, IJOE
JNBO IH VONBO IJNI QZNKG
HAIPKRO, NGR BHIO TAPI NP
IJOKZ VONROZP IOVV'OW IH.
　　　C.P. LKVQOZI (KHVNGIJO)

Now try to find a keyed phrase (7,7) connected with the cryptogram. Against each letter of plain text (column 1) write its encoded form (column 2). Then, against each letter of code text (column 3) write its plain text form (column 4). You will find that some letters in column 4 are in alphabetical order; the letters that are not are those that make up the key phrase. They appear in their correct order, although, of course, repeated letters have been omitted and must be replaced. A little imagination is needed to work out the hidden phrase – for instance, ANPLEDY would be all that would appear of 'an apple a day'.

Cryptokey 2

Using the same rules explained in Q103, solve the following cryptogram and then find a further keyed message (7, 8).

YWLH PIOYPNGO L IJKGCJNKUH
JBLKPJI, PS YGNSJNXGN
SAWSPWO GDYGMKLKPJI, LIH
KHYG TGKO L ULIR, IPIG-SJJK
JIGO LNG NGLW TNLIR; JAK JS
KAIG, LWW FGH 'WPOEK'IGNO'
SNAOKNLKPJI.

NAKU Q. LWKXLI

1	2	3	4
A		A	
B		B	
C		C	
D		D	
E		E	
F		F	
G		G	
H		H	
I		I	
J		J	
K		K	
L		L	
M		M	
N		N	
O		O	
P		P	
Q		Q	
R		R	
S		S	
T		T	
U		U	
V		V	
W		W	
X		X	
Y		Y	
Z		Z	

Cryptokey 3

Using the same rules explained in Q103 solve the following cryptogram and then find a further keyed message (11, 6).

EKJ, CGY TNZI RIOKPIJNXIOC XNEXIR XAG ATGOI AGJLE; CGY TNZI TKEEIR NOO LC LCEXIJC OIQXYJIE NHR PIIH QNYMTX SKMTXKHM N OKNJ KH XTI WYNR; CGY AKOO FOINEI OINZI GBSGJR PC XTI HIBX XGAH RJNKH.

	1	2	3	4
A		A		
B		B		
C		C		
D		D		
E		E		
F		F		
G		G		
H		H		
I		I		
J		J		
K		K		
L		L		
M		M		
N		N		
O		O		
P		P		
Q		Q		
R		R		
S		S		
T		T		
U		U		
V		V		
W		W		
X		X		
Y		Y		
Z		Z		

CROSSWORD VARIATIONS

Crossword puzzles are probably the most favoured of all word games, and they are attempted every day by millions of people. The person generally credited with the invention of the modern crossword puzzle was Arthur Wynne, an Englishman from Liverpool, who emigrated to New York and whose first crossword puzzle, originally called a Word Cross puzzle, appeared in the Sunday newspaper, the *New York World* in 1913. The crossword craze had started, and the first book of crosswords was published by the US publishers Simon & Schuster in 1924. In 1925 a Broadway revue, *Puzzles of 1925,* included a scene set in a 'Crossword Puzzle Sanatorium' for people who had been driven insane by their infatuation and obsession with this new craze.

Hardly surprising then, that a few of the pseudonyms of some of the great crossword compilers of this century are Torquemada, Ximenes and Azed (Deza in reverse), the names of leaders of the Spanish Inquisition!

All the puzzles in this section are spin-offs from the traditional crossword and they are designed to tease and torment rather than to drive you mad with frustration and desperation.

Criss-cross Word

Answers run horizontally, vertically, or diagonally, either to right or left. Each solution starts on the lower number and finishes on the next higher number – 1 to 2, 2 to 3 and so on.

Clues:

1. Swiss singing
2. Inarticulate sounds
3. Brilliantly lit spot
4. Perceptible to touch
5. Enclosure for letter
6. Devoted to pleasure
7. Location
8. Rub out

9. Passes
10. Thermoplastic resin
11 . Introducer
12 . Give out
13. Sets of three
14. Pouch
15. Young horse
16. Slender
17. Fresh

1	5						4
10		13			12		7
	17					15	
						14	
			16				
11		8			9		6
3							2

Seven-letter Words

Fill in the nine letters in the centre of the crossword to produce eight seven-letter words, each travelling in the direction of an arrow.

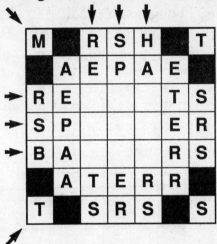

Nursery Rhyme Crossword

Pussy cat, one of the cat families, where have you been? I've been to London where the queen lives, avoiding hazards. Pussy cat, pussy cat, what did you do there? I bought some ladies' frocks for my female family, and frightened a little mouse under a chair, who was quite genuine, but did not agree to keep quiet.

In the above narrative are eight clues. Find them, solve them and enter the answers in the grid to complete the crossword.

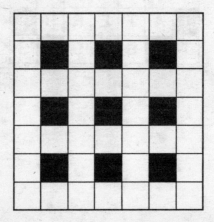

Alphabet Crossword

Complete the grid by placing all 26 letters of the alphabet in the circles. Use each letter once only.

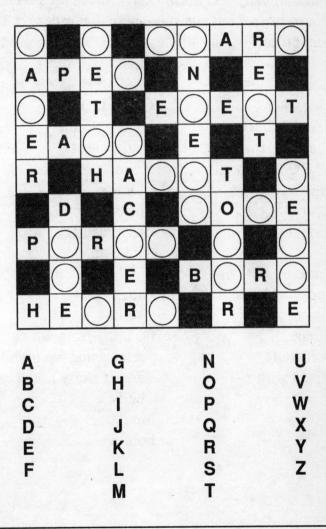

A		G		N		U
B		H		O		V
C		I		P		W
D		J		Q		X
E		K		R		Y
F		L		S		Z
		M		T		

Here are four connected 5 × 5 magic word squares. In each grid the five five-letter words can be read both vertically and horizontally. Clues are given in groups of five but are in no particular order within each group.

Clues 1-5
Hair on chin
The sacred writings of the Christian religion
Big
Senior
Perfect

Clues 6- 10 :
Burn surface of
Moist
Pursue
Bordered
Mixed with

Clues 11-15:
High IQ-society
Eagle's nest
Animals of the cat family
The crime of a pyromaniac
Kingdom

Clues 16-20:
Useful
Quantity from which results may be found
Largest artery in the body
Men
Follow

No Blanks

Place the 20 words in the grid so that a word can be read on each horizontal and vertical line. You have to work out which words go horizontally and which go vertically.

CAB	TIRED	MALES
WAN	JAPES	BARED
DOMED	CORES	NET
WOMEN	COMET	BED
DOPES	PALED	
BORED	SIREN	
TOMES	PARES	
CARED	SORES	

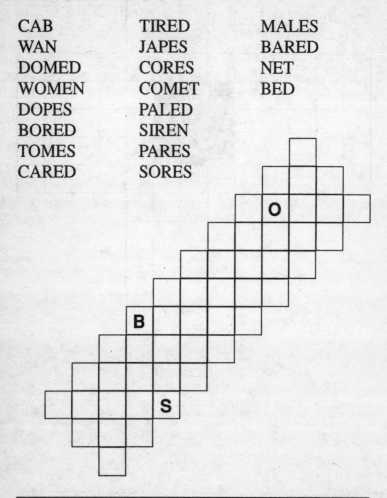

WIND-UPS

We wind up this latest collection of puzzles with another pot pourri to test and tease you, but, we hope, not wind you up too much.

We hope you found the puzzles enjoyable and were able to come up with many of the answers. For the puzzles that you were unable to crack, you should find that the explanations provided will give you a clear idea of what you should have done to come up with the correct solution.

Good luck and keep puzzling!

Colours

Each horizontal and vertical line contains the letters of a colour, but the letters are jumbled. Find 20 colours. Every letter is used, but only once each.

M	E	L	W	U	O	E	O	L	N
E	U	P	P	L	E	R	T	P	A
D	A	Y	B	E	C	A	A	C	N
E	E	K	C	S	T	R	I	S	E
E	R	A	R	Z	A	R	V	U	V
H	I	N	W	L	T	Y	E	R	U
E	N	R	N	G	G	B	E	E	E
R	B	U	R	B	A	B	L	A	Y
D	G	I	O	L	N	O	I	T	M
I	M	R	N	C	M	O	E	M	S

Three Names

Can you think of three familiar given or first names that, when written down in any order, will form a meaningful sentence?

Three Words 2

You are looking for three words to answer this riddle:

Speak not in haste, mere hesitation,
Does headless appear in sound vexation,
Lest he at first complete is heard,
And read aloud will find my word.

Professions/Occupations

Complete the following, which are all professions or occupations. Then re-arrange the first letters of each to find a tenth occupation.

```
.A.I.L.G.S.        .E.S.A.T.R
.T.O.N.Y           .N.E.T.R
.O.K.M.T.          .R.N.O.G.R
.E.F.A.E.          .I.G.A.T.R
.R.H.T.C.
```

Matchsticks

Fifty-seven matchsticks are laid out below to form a sum that is obviously incorrect. Remove just three of the matchsticks to make the sum correct.

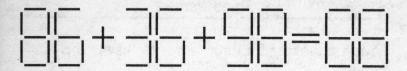

Neologisms

A neologism is a newly coined word or phrase or a familiar word that is used in a new way. In the grid are 15 such words, which can be found horizontally, diagonally or vertically, backwards or forwards, but always in a straight line. Can you find them with the help of the clues provided?

Clues:

1. Robbery in crowded places
2. Prolonged traffic jam
3. An unstated message
4. Record a credit card
5. Small shops in one building
6. Having full ability
7. A signature
8. Surge of euphoria
9. Of a very bright shade
10. Chemical used by fruit growers
11. Woman's one-piece garment
12. Unsolicited telephone call
13. Plastic card with information stored on it
14. Graphical user interface (abbreviation)
15. Electronic musical keyboard

K	T	X	E	T	B	U	S
C	R	A	A	C	R	T	W
O	A	C	G	K	E	Y	I
L	I	U	D	A	S	Y	P
D	I	H	M	E	A	D	E
I	Y	I	S	G	L	O	X
R	N	A	H	U	A	B	Y
G	A	L	L	E	R	I	A

Odd One Out

Which of the following words is the odd one out?

Corn
Area
Bite
Cube
Aura

Fruit

How many cherries are needed to make scale B balance?

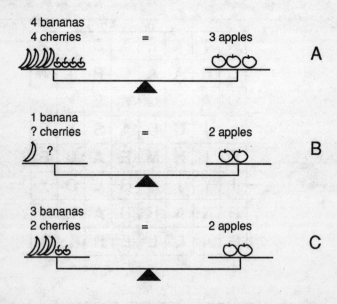

4 bananas
4 cherries = 3 apples   A

1 banana
? cherries = 2 apples   B

3 bananas
2 cherries = 2 apples   C

ANSWERS

A1	Murphy's Twelfth Law	Q54

You can not lead a cavalry charge if you think you look funny on a horse.

A2	Sharon's Telegram	Q91

Read the end of the sentence backwards: 'Marge lets Norah.'

A3	Return Journey	Q37

30 mph. Let the car's speed = x mph; then the increased speed = $x + 5$ mph.

Journey time at original speed = $210 \div x$ hours

Journey time at increased speed = $210 \div (x + 5)$ hours

Therefore,

$$(210 \div x) - (210 \div (x + 5)) = 1$$

Multiply each side by x then by $x + 5$:

$$210(x + 5) - 210x = x(x + 5)$$
$$= x^2 + 5x - 1050 = 0$$
$$= 30 \text{ or } -35$$

Because -35 is a negative speed, the original speed must have been 30 mph.

A4	Three Words 2	Q114

Stutter, tutter, utter – 'lest he', read quickly, sounds like 'less t' (tutter, less t = utter).

A5	Fraction	Q40

$$\frac{3942}{15768}$$

A6	Anagram Magic Square	Q65

S	A	T	I	N
A	R	E	N	A
T	E	L	L	S
I	N	L	E	T
N	A	S	T	Y

204 – i.e., $8^2 + 7^2 + 6^2 + 5^2 + 4^2 + 3^2 + 2^2 + 1^2$

Bill. Let a equal the amount that Alan had and let b equal the amount that Bill had before Alan and Bill bet. Then, from (1), after they had bet:

$$\text{Alan} = 2a$$
$$\text{Bill} = b - a$$

Let c be the amount Charlie had before he bet with Bill. Then, from (2), after Bill and Charlie bet:

$$\text{Bill} = (b - a) + (b - a)$$
$$= 2b - 2a$$
$$\text{Charlie} = c - (b - a)$$
$$= c - b + a$$

Then, from (3), after Charlie and Alan bet:

$$\text{Charlie} = (c - b + a) + (c - b + a)$$
$$= 2c - 2b + 2a$$
$$\text{Alan} = 2a - (c - b + a)$$
$$= a - c + b$$

From (4): $a - c + b = 2b - 2a$

and, $a - c + b = 2c - 2b + 2a$

The first equation yields: $b = 3a - c$

The second equation yields: $3b = a + 3c$

Therefore, $6b = 10a$

$$b = 5a/3$$

Substituting for b: $c = 4a/3$

If Alan had started with £x, Bill would have started with £$5x/3$ and Charlie would have started with £$4x/3$. However, Alan cannot have started with £50; otherwise Bill and Charlie would have started with fractions of a pound. If Bill started with £50, Alan would have started with £30 and Charlie would have started with £40.

W, or, you, turn, goose, voodoo, terrify, fleeting, yodelling

A10	Decimals	Q93

2.646 – the square root of 7. The numbers are the square roots of 1, 2, 3, 4, 5 and 6.

A11	Consonants	Q27

1. Festivity; 2. Amusement; 3. Conviviality; 4. Jollification; 5. Merriment; 6. Pleasure; 7. Revelry; 8. Gaiety; 8. Joviality.

A12	Alphabetical Sequence	Q8

Move 'abysmal' from last to first. The first and last letters of the words spell the word 'alphabetical'.

A13	Nursery Rhyme Crossword	Q108

A14	Trackwords	Q21

1. Unparliamentary; 2. Manoeuvrability

A15	Rebuses 1	Q72

1. Big top; 2. Tin foil; 3. The ayes to the right, the noes to the left;
4. A piece of cake; 5. A turn-up for the book; 6. Mixed fortunes;
7. Onion; 8. Striptease; 9. Scatterbrain; 10 Sitting target;
11. Short-handed; 12. A leaf out of someone's book

A16	Four Numbers	Q2

4, 7, 9 and 11

A17	Network 2	Q24

Verisimilitude

A18   Silli Billis   Q97

In Roman numerals: MCCOI = comic

A19   Cann's Axiom   Q48

When all else fails, read the instructions.

A20   Fruit   Q119

Six cherries. Let apples be a, bananas b and cherries c, then take scale
C $(3b + 2c = 2a)$ from scale A $(4b + 4c = 3a)$:
$$b + 2c = a$$
$$\text{therefore, } 2b + 4c = 2a$$
$$\text{but, } 3b + 2c = 2a \text{ (scale C)}$$
$$\text{therefore, } 2b + 4c = 3b + 2c$$
$$b = 2c$$
Substituting two of the three bananas on scale C with four cherries,
gives one banana and six cherries on scale B.

A21   Four Letters   Q77

CDEN – they are the first letters of the States of the USA in alphabetical
order, followed by the first three letters of the State capital: Alabama –
Montgomery; Alaska – Juneau; Arizona – Phoenix; Arkansas – Little
Rock; California – Sacramento; Colorado – Denver.

A22   Containers   Q13

1. La(burn)um; 2. C(ape)r; 3. A(lame)in; 4. Fi(rear)m; 5. V(ale)ta;
6. Sch(nap)ps; 7. Me(ring)ue; 8. La(cross)e; 9. C(level)and;
10. Swe(etc)orn

A23   Sixers   Q26

1. Aerial; 2. Otiose; 3. Oedema; 4. Eyelid; 5. Louvre; 6. Irrupt

A24   Agnes's Law   Q49

Almost everything in life is easier to get into than out of.

A25 Replace the Vowels Q10

To step into another man's shoes.

A26 Topiary Q98

Turn the page upside down and read between the hedges to discover
the message 'Go away'.

A27 Neologisms Q117

1. Steaming; 2. Gridlock; 3. Subtext; 4. Swipe; 5. Galleria; 6. Abled;
7. Tag; 8. Rush; 9. Acid; 10. Alar; 11. Body; 12. Cold; 13. Laser;
14. GUI; 15. Key

A28 Cryptosymbol Q102

Government, even in its best state, is but a necessary evil; in its worst
state, an intolerable one. Tom Paine

A29 Alphabet Crossword Q109

A30 The Lake Q95

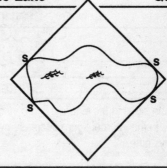

A31   No Zeros   Q78

$1{,}000{,}000{,}000 = 10^9 = 2^9 \times 5^9 = 512 \times 1953125$

A32   Paths   Q28

252

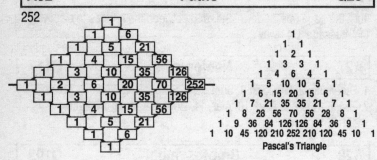

Pascal's Triangle

A33   Round Table   Q39

720. The first choice of position at a circular table is made at random, and the subsequent choices are made in relation to the first. When the first member has sat down wherever he or she pleases, the next member has six choices, the third has five choices and so on. Therefore, $6! = 6 \times 5 \times 4 \times 3 \times 2 \times 1 = 720$.

A34   Hexagonal Connections   Q23

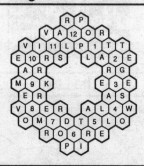

A35   Sequence   Q56

B – the sides in the external figure increase by one each time, while the sides in the internel figure decrease by one. Also, the total of the sides is always nine.

A36   The Enigmasig Wheel   Q66

Negate (invalidate); integrate (amalgamate); gullible (credulous); morose (depressed); assurance (affirmation); swathe (enwrap); inspire (stimulate); gaze (contemplate)

A37   Five Words   Q96

3 – the remaining groups contain the same 24 letters, which, incidentally, can be arranged to form the sentence: 'Re-arrange all these letters.'

A38   No-repeat letters 1   Q16

Soundtrack

A39   Anagrammed Synonyms   Q64

1. Din – uproar; 2. Rub – abrade; 3. Hoax – deception; 4. Drop – globule: 5. Lone – isolated; 6. Saw – aphorism; Stud – bespangle; 8. Way – procedure; 9. Note – epistle; 10. Tie – restrain

A40   Rebuses 2   Q73

1. Three-point turn; 2. Furlong; 3. A pig in a poke; 4. Spotted dick; 5. On the top; 6. Sleep like a log; 7. Well-informed; 8. Example; 9. Middle-English; 10. Corner shop; 11. Fall back; 12. Skin-deep

A41   Railway Wagon   Q99

The wagon will move to the right and stop. Let A be the centre of gravity of the empty wagon **and** the centre of gravity of the wagon when the valve is open; let B be the centre of gravity of the wagon before the valve is opened; let C be the centre of gravity of the water section before the valve is opened; let D be the point below the centre of gravity before the valve is opened; and let E be the point beneath A. When the water has evenly filled the wagon, the centre of gravity will move to E.

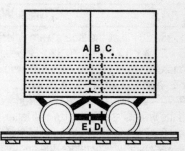

A42   Palindromic Sequence   Q87

4 – change the numbers to Roman numerals: VI, IX, II, IV, I, VIII, XI, IV.

A43   No Blanks   Q111

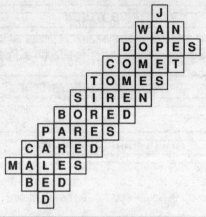

A44   Professions/Occupations   Q115

Radiologist, attorney, locksmith, beefeater, architect, newscaster, inventor, ironmonger, ringmaster. Anagram: librarian.

A45   Train Trip   Q1

95 people paid £41 each.

A46   Network 1   Q15

Scintillating

A47   Three Words 1   Q42

1. 35,280 – if all the letters were different the answer would be 8!: 8 x 7 x 6 x 5 x 4 x 3 x 2 x 1 = 40,320. However, we must allow for the interchange of the two As, which would appear the same, by deducting one-eighth of 40,320 – i.e., 5,040.

2. 72 – the five letters can be arranged in 5! ways: 5 x 4 x 3 x 2 x = 120. If the vowels are treated as one letter, the number of arrangements is 4!: 4 x 3 x 2 x 1 = 24, but in each of these the vowels can be arranged as either ou or uo. Therefore, the number of arrangements in which the

vowels are together is 2 x 24 = 48, and the number of arrangements in which the vowels are separated is 120 – 48.

3. 720 – the seven letters can be arranged in 7! ways: 7 x 6 x 5 x 4 x 3 x 2 x 1 = 5,040. However, we must deduct from this total 6 x 5 x 2 x 3 x 4! = 4,320.

A48	Sea Level	Q79

3 miles – the eyes have to be $2n^2 \div 3$ feet above sea level to see n miles out to sea. Therefore, $2n^2 \div 3 = 6$; $2n^2 = 18$; $n^2 = 9$; $n = 3$.

A49	Blomgren's Law	Q55

Reality is a hypothesis.

A50	Two Hexagons	Q59

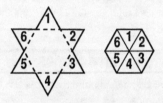

A51	Two Numbers	Q3

98 and 94

A52	Codeword	Q6

Remain

```
4 6 5          1 2 3 4 5 6        3   2 1
BELONG        (RUMBLE)         ARMOUR
4 6 5          1 2 3 4 5 6        3   2 1
ANIMAL        (REMAIN)         CAMBER
```

A53	Coins	Q31

First purchase:

Second purchase:

△ + ▢   ▢ + ○

A54	Dominoes	Q81

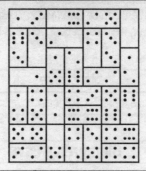

A55	Prime Numbers	Q88

None – the nine digits add up to 45, which is divisible by 3. This means that the number itself is divisible by 3, and in whatever way the digits are arranged, they will always total 45 so that the numbers themselves will also always be divisible by 3.

A56	Three Names	Q113

Pat Sue, Bill; Pat, sue Bill; Pat, bill Sue; Sue, pat Bill; Sue, bill Pat; Bill, sue Pat; Bill, pat Sue.

A57	The 20 10-letter Word Boggle	Q86

Auditorium, vulnerable, disappoint, worthwhile, boisterous, orchestral, journalism, illuminate, proprietor, particular, bedeviled, psychology, formidable, optimistic, turbulence, quadrangle, remarkable, scholastic, determined, excitement

A58	Numbergram	Q101

Work expands so as to fill the time available for its completion.

Cyril Northcote Parkinson

A59	Colours	Q112

Across: lemon, purple, cyan, cerise, azure, white, green, ruby, gold, crimson
Down: red, amber, pink, brown, blue, magenta, bay, violet, scarlet, mauve

A60   Magic Square   Q36

17	6	12	8	22
24	13	14	9	5
11	7	1	25	21
3	23	18	19	2
10	16	20	4	15

A61   Scrabble   Q11

Intrinsic

A62   Odd One Out   Q118

Area – the other words are formed from two sets of chemical symbols: Corn (Co = cobalt, Rn = radon); Bite (Bi = bismuth; Te = tellurium); Cube (Cu = Copper, Be = beryllium); Aura (Au = gold; Ra = radium). Area has an element in the first half only – Ar = argon.

A63   Hexagonal Pyramid   Q61

D – lines that are in common in the two hexagons immediately below a hexagon are cancelled out, but lines that appear in only one of the hexagons are carried forwards.

A64   Key Sequence   Q94

Cleft – turn the keys upside down and read the word formed by the lock ends.

A65   Gumperson's Law   Q53

The probability of anything happening is in inverse proportion to its desirability.

A66   Keyword   Q4

Newspaper – 1–4 = news; 4–6 = spa; 6–8 = ape; 1–3 = new; 5–9 = paper

A67   Bracket Word   Q14

Phonetically

Misfortune

Place the information in a chart:

	Frib	Twog	Gluc	Shen	Korl	Brut
Caln			no			✓
Dork		✓			no	
Josh	✓		no		✓	✓
Loji	no			✓		
Mith	no		✓			
Nurf	✓	✓		✓	no	

Korl is a Josh; therefore, Frib must be a Nurf; Twog must be a Dork; Shen must be a Loji; Brut must be a Caln; and, by elimination, Gluc must be a Mith.

The cube of 4464658829 ends in 0123456789, and the cube of 871517841 ends in 0987654321.

Give me the luxuries of life and I will willingly do without the necessities.   Frank Lloyd Wright

Turn

Ambidextrous

5	x	2	-	6	=	4
+		x		÷		x
3	+	4	+	2	=	9
÷		÷		-		÷
4	x	2	-	2	=	6
=		=		=		=
2	+	4	÷	1	=	6

A75	**Cryptokey 2**	Q104

Play inspires a noteworthy ovation,/If performer fulfils expectation,/Any type gets a hand,/Nine-foot ones are real grand;/Out of tune, all key 'Liszt' ners' frustration.   Ruth B. Altman

Keyed phrase: Keynote acrostic (KEYNOTACRSI); look at the initial letters of the words in the first line and of the first words of each line.

A76	**Reserves**	Q7

40 minutes – (50 x 8) ÷ 10

A77	**No-repeat Letters 3**	Q18

Palindrome

A78	**Anagram Phrases**	Q68

1. To bring to light; 2. To drop like a hot potato; 3. To break the ice; 4. Seven deadly sins; 5. Birds of a feather

---

A79	**Finagle's Law and Chisholme's Law**	Q51

Once a job is fouled up, everything done to improve it only makes it worse (Finagle's Law). Any time things appear to be going better, you have overlooked something (Chisholme's Law).

A80	**Gee Whiz!**	Q20

1. Goldfinch; 2. Gangplank; 3. Governess; 4. Generator; 5. Gymnasium; 6. Gestation; 7. Galloping; 8. Garibaldi; 9. Gladstone

E – looking both across and down, if two circles appear in the same position in the first two squares, they are carried forwards to the third square in the same position, but they change from black to white or from white to black. If only one circle appears in a given position, it, too, is carried forwards to the third square, but it does not change colour.

They can all be read in a straight line – horizontally, vertically and diagonally – on a standard calculator key-pad.

To produce the words: resorts, sputter, halters, results, spotter, barters, masters and tartlet.

1. 266 – 2783 x 4 = 11132; 1113 x 2 = 2226; 222 x 6 = 1332; 133 x 2 = 266
2. 281 – the numbers are produced by taking the digits 843, re-arranging them in every possible combination and dividing each in turn by 3.
3. 420 – they are times without the full point, with 25 minutes added each time: 1.25, 1.50, 2.15, 2.40 and so on.

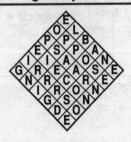

A86	No-repeat Letters 4	Q19

Valedictory

A87	Analogy	Q58

A – the lines in the two figures are added together, except for those lines they have in common.

A88	Matchsticks	Q116

66 - 36 + 58 = 88

A89	Rebuses 3	Q74

1. Excuse; 2 Low frequency; 3. Indecent; 4. Cornerstone; 5. Neon light; 6. Shortbread; 7. The height of passion; 8. Snake in the grass; 9. Well-connected; 10. Much ado about nothing; 11. Checkpoint; 12. To lie in state

A90	Cricketers	Q34

David = 10; Mike = 12; Graham = 9

A91	Quartering a Square	Q57

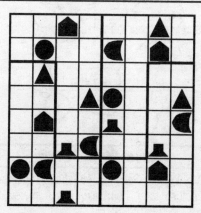

1	2	3	4	5
C	E	A	B	D

H	F	I	J	G
10	9	8	7	6

Mar – the words are the first three letters of States in the USA:
Washington, Tennessee, Pennsylvania and Maryland.

Add the 10 weights together (1,156kg) and divide by four to give the
total weight of all five contestants – i.e., 289kg. If the contestants are
called A, B, C, D and E in ascending order of weight, A + B must weigh
IIOkg and D + E must weigh 121kg; therefore, C weighs 289 – (110 +
121)kg = 58kg, which makes it possible to determine the other weights:
A = 54kg; B = 56kg; C = 58kg; D = 59kg; E = 62kg.

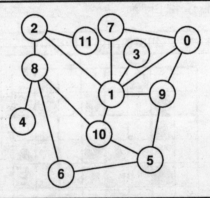

Lord of the Flies by William Golding, 1954. Leery, opprobrium, raptorial,
dulse, ortolan, fructose, tamp, houri, exordium, furbelow, lox, impetigo,
eyrir, slough

A97   Jumble   Q25

Wheresoever, whistlestop, workmanlike, watercolour, worldliness, witchhunter, wintergreen, weighbridge

A98   Island   Q33

A = 'truber', B = 'fibber' and C = 'truer'. Suppose that B's statement were true. Then A's statement would be true, and C would be a 'truer'. However, this cannot be possible, because it would mean that all three had made true statements. Therefore, B's statement is false, and A is not a 'truer'. It follows that neither A nor B is a 'truer', so C must be a 'truer'. A's statement is true, so A must be a 'truber', and B must be a 'fibber'.

A99   Rebuses 4   Q75

1. Stick insect; 2. Spread eagle; 3. Chairperson; 4. At a loose end; 5. In two minds; 6. Court circular; 7. Close harmony; 8. Stop watch; 9. T square; 10. A quarter of an hour; 11. Split level; 12. All in all

A100   Pyramid Words 1   Q69

A, in, ton, city, field – confidentiality

A101   16 Letters   Q82

The 16 letters in each section can be re-arranged into the words 'a well known phrase'.

A102   The 38 Puzzle   Q43

A103　　　　Square Numbers　　　　Q46

Across: 5184, 1764, 3721, 9604, 1225, 4225, 8836, 6561
Down: 2116, 6889, 5329, 1369, 4624, 3136, 9216, 3481

A104　　　　Anagram Themes　　　　Q71

1. The theme is trees: cherry (cry, her); chestnut (cuts, then); laburnum (album, run); maple (me, lap); poplar (rap, lop); redwood (ode, word); sycamore (cosy, mare)
2. The theme is girls' names: Belinda (bail, end); Brenda (bar, den); Heather (hear, the); Miranda (maid, ran); Muriel (lie, rum); Sheila (sail, he); Thelma (elm, hat)

A105　　　　Ages　　　　Q44

1. Children 4, 15 and 20; wife 39
2. Daughters 10, 12 and 15; myself 37

A106　　　　Ponemon's Provocation　　　　Q50

If you do not know who is to blame, you are. Start with the I between the B and N, then take every third letter clockwise.

AI07　　　　Matrix 2　　　　Q62

G – the lines in the two preceding figures, horizontally and vertically, are added together, except for those lines they have in common.

A108　　　　Pyramid Words 2　　　　Q70

E, no, nut, slay, stain – instantaneously

A109　　　　Cartwheels　　　　Q83

Front wheel = 15 feet, rear wheel = 18 feet.

　　　360ft ÷ 24 = 15ft }
　　　360ft ÷ 20 = 18ft } difference is four revolutions

When the circumferences are reduced by 3 feet:

　　　360ft ÷ 30 = 12ft }
　　　360ft ÷ 24 = 15ft } difference is six revolutions

A110   Coal Overboard   Q92

Fall – the coal displaces more water in the barge (its weight) than in the water (its volume).

A111   Cryptokey 1   Q103

When in that house MPs divide,/If they've a brain and cerebellum too,/They have to leave that brain outside,/And vote just as their leaders tell 'em to.   W.S. Gilbert, *Iolanthe*

Keyed phrase: Nothing changes (NOTHIGCAES)

A112   Criss-cross Word   Q106

1. yodelling; 2. gibberish; 3. highlight; 4. tangible; 5. envelope;
6. epicure; 7. emplace; 8. erase; 9. elapses; 10. shellac; 11. compere;
12. emit; 13. trios; 14. sac; 15. colt; 16. thin; 17. new

A113   Feldstein's Law   Q52

Never ever play leapfrog with unicorns.

A114   Hexagons   Q63

B – the black circle moves clockwise one section, then two sections, then three sections, etc.; the black triangle moves clockwise two sections, then one section, then two sections, etc.; the white triangle moves anticlockwise one section, then two sections, then three sectfons, etc.; the white circle moves anticlockwise one section, then two sections, then three sections, etc.

A115   Squares?   Q45

Although only four of the six numbers appear to be squares, they are, in fact, all squares. Each term is 100 expressed in a different base:
$100_{10} = 121_9 = 144_8 = 202_7 = 244_6 = 400_5 = 1210_4$

A116   Rebuses 5   Q76

1. Wheels within wheels; 2. High noon; 3. A state of confusion;
4. A change of policy; 5. Inland revenue; 6. Storm centre; 7. Streets apart; 8. Platinum; 9. Space suit; 10. Centre of gravity; 11. Cardinal;
12. The Fifth Amendment

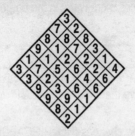

Sir, you have deliberately tasted two whole worms; you have hissed all my mystery lectures and been caught fighting a liar in the quad; you will please leave Oxford by the next town drain. Keyed phrase: Spoonerisms galore (SPONERIMGAL)

1. Bible, 2. ideal, 3. beard, 4. large, 5. elder, 6. chase, 7. humid, 8. among, 9. singe, 10. edged, 11. realm, 12. eyrie, 13. arson, 14. lions, 15. Mensa, 16. datum, 17. aorta, 18. trail, 19. utile, 20. males